Mindfulness Meditation for Beginners

Master and Kick Out Anxiety and Depression With Guided Mindfulness Meditation

(How to Calm the Mind and Live Stress Free)

George Gist

Published by Rob Miles

© **George Gist**

All Rights Reserved

Mindfulness Meditation for Beginners: Master and Kick Out Anxiety and Depression With Guided Mindfulness Meditation (How to Calm the Mind and Live Stress Free)

ISBN 978-1-989990-88-9

All rights reserved. No part of this guide may be reproduced in any form without permission in writing from the publisher except in the case of brief quotations embodied in critical articles or reviews.

LEGAL & DISCLAIMER

The information contained in this book is not designed to replace or take the place of any form of medicine or professional medical advice. The information in this book has been provided for educational and entertainment purposes only.

The information contained in this book has been compiled from sources deemed reliable, and it is accurate to the best of the Author's knowledge; however, the Author cannot guarantee its accuracy and validity and cannot be held liable for any errors or omissions. Changes are periodically made to this book. You must consult your doctor or get professional medical advice before using any of the suggested remedies, techniques, or information in this book.

Upon using the information contained in this book, you agree to hold harmless the Author from and against any damages, costs, and expenses, including any legal fees potentially resulting from the application of any of the information provided by this guide. This disclaimer applies to any damages or injury caused by the use and application, whether directly or indirectly, of any advice or information presented, whether for breach of contract, tort, negligence, personal injury, criminal intent, or under any other cause of action.

You agree to accept all risks of using the information presented inside this book. You need to consult a professional medical practitioner in order to ensure you are both able and healthy enough to participate in this program.

Table of Contents

INTRODUCTION 1

CHAPTER 1: WHAT EXACTLY IS MINDFULNESS AND WHY SHOULD I BOTHER? 4

CHAPTER 2: MEDITATION 23

CHAPTER 3: BENEFITS OF MINDFULNESS 33

CHAPTER 4: THE 8 ATTITUDES THAT DEFINES A MINDFUL HEART. 45

CHAPTER 5: POWERFUL STEPS TO SELF-LOVE 57

CHAPTER 6: CALM THE MIND 67

CHAPTER 7: MEDITATION TIPS AND TECHNIQUES 81

CHAPTER 8: BE MINDFUL EVERYDAY 85

CHAPTER 9: MINDFUL THOUGHTS: YOU REALLY NEED TO SLOW DOWN 98

CHAPTER 10: BEING MINDFUL OF YOUR THOUGHTS .. 110

CHAPTER 11: BENEFITS OF MINDFULNESS 122

CHAPTER 12: MINDFULNESS AND THERAPY 131

CHAPTER 13: MINDFULNESS TECHNIQUES FOR STRESS, ANXIETY AND DEPRESSION RELIEF 144

CHAPTER 14. HOW TO PRACTICE MINDFULNESS MEDITATION FOR STRESS RELIEF 150

CHAPTER 15: MINDFUL EXERCISES UNDER 10 MINUTES TO 30 MINUTES 173

CHAPTER 16: THE DIFFERENCE BETWEEN MEDITATION AND MINDFULNESS 187

CONCLUSION 200

Introduction

As you go through the motions of your busy day, how much attention do you really pay to the things you are doing? When you drive the kids to school, are you actively paying attention to your driving and to other drivers on the road or are you thinking about what you need to do when you get to the office? As you fold laundry at home are you focused on the task or are you already planning in your head what you are going to cook for dinner? It is very easy to multi-task in your mind, thinking about the next task before you even finish the one at-hand but this type of thinking can lead to stress, anxiety, and other problems.

Rather than turning your mind always toward the next thing, consider what it might be like if you were to focus instead on what you are doing in the moment. Paying attention to the actions you are taking and the thoughts you are having will help you to live in the moment and to be more connected to the details of your daily life. This practice is called "mindfulness" and it simply involves focusing your attention on the present.

Mindfulness is an ancient practice that originated with Buddhist monks and it plays an important role in modern meditation practices. Practicing mindfulness not only improves your concentration and mental focus, but it can actually have some very real benefits for your physical and mental wellbeing. In this book you will learn the basics about what mindfulness is, where it comes from, and how it can benefit you. You will also receive detailed instructions for practicing mindfulness on your own in order to relieve stress and anxiety, to reduce feelings of depression, and to achieve many more benefits. If you are ready to take back control of your mind, turn the page and keep reading!

CHAPTER 1: WHAT EXACTLY IS MINDFULNESS AND WHY SHOULD I BOTHER?

WHAT MINDFULNESS IS

Mindfulness is, quite simply, "Paying attention to present moment experience with open curiosity and a willingness to be with what is."[1]

Let's just take that definition apart a bit at a time. Paying attention. This is possibly the hardest part of mindfulness training. Paying attention to anything in a world with so many competing demands can seem like an impossibility. Do you pay attention when you're eating or do you shovel in your lunch at the same time as reading a report, or watching TV, or chatting with co-workers? Do you pay attention to your kids when they want to show you their latest work of art when you've got dinner to prepare and the phone is ringing and the dog's just been sick on the kitchen floor?

Probably not. Many wonderful and uplifting things in life happen while tons of other 'stuff' is happening all around us. We miss out on those potentially life-enhancing moments because we are out of practice at paying attention.

Present moment experience. The next part of the definition shows us what it is exactly we are missing out on. We are missing the Right Now. Not a few moments ago, not a couple of minutes into the future. Right Now. The present moment is life's gift to us, and mindfulness is about learning to pay attention to all that gift has to offer.

Open curiosity is in itself a curious term when you first come across it. What does it mean, exactly? I like to think of it as becoming more like a child. Children have a magical open curiosity – they are literally curious about everything. No distinctions are made between so-called interesting or uninteresting facts or experiences; in the young child's eyes it's all equal and it's all equally fascinating.

The final part of our basic definition calls for "a willingness to be with what is." Do you have that willingness? I know I didn't when I first discovered mindfulness. I had a willingness to get the bills paid, to complete my To Do list, to get the house cleaned and get the kids to their after school clubs on time. I had a willingness to make my life better, not be with it how it is.

And this, along with paying attention, is probably the hardest part. A willingness to be with what is requires what is perhaps similar to a leap of faith. It's about being non-judgmental, and accepting yourself exactly as you are, as well as accepting the world around you.

Mindfulness is contrasted with states of mind in which attention is focussed elsewhere, for example a pre-occupation with memories, fantasies of the future, plans or worries, and of behaving automatically without awareness of your actions.

History and background

Mindfulness is based on an Eastern meditation tradition, but it is not dependent on any belief or ideology. The word 'mindfulness' is a translation of the Indian word, Sati, which means awareness, attention and remembering. These principles have been applied in human practices, disciplines and religions for thousands and thousands of years; solving human problems with intrinsic awareness and inner resources is at the heart of many ancient teachings. Daoism concerns itself with developing a harmonious relationship between humans and the world by contemplating the "ground of existence", while Buddhist mindfulness centers on sitting meditations and mindfulness of the breath. Mindfulness practices and principles can be found in Hinduism, Muslim traditions and Christianity, and in movement meditations such as yoga and tai chi.

Today, however, mindfulness has evolved into a more secular discipline, partly through the work of Jon Kabat-Zinn and his Mindfulness-Based Stress Reduction (MBSR) program, which he launched at the University of Massachusetts Medical School in 1979. So, although many of the principles can also be applied to ancient teachings, you certainly do not have to be religious in any way to enjoy the benefits of regular practice.

Mindfulness meditation

The meditation part of mindfulness practice is something that puts many people off, at least initially . As soon as they hear the word 'meditate' they get an image in their minds of having to sit in the lotus position, perhaps while burning incense and playing music with the tinkling of little bells in the background ...

Mindfulness meditation does not need to be like this at all, as I hope you've already experienced for yourself by now after taking 3 minutes out to practice the first guided meditation at the start of this chapter. If you didn't take a time-out to do it then, I really hope you will right now. Remember, the only way to get a new habit is to take new actions, and the way to mindfulness is to practice, practice, practice. More on that later in the book.

Traditional meditation is more formal, often allied to a particular teaching, such as Buddhism. Mindfulness meditation, however, is more free-flowing, and open to personal interpretation. As you'll see from the guided mindfulness mediations in this book, you can practice mindfulness while sitting, walking, eating, playing, or simply while doing absolutely nothing.

Simple but not necessarily easy!

In that case, it's a breeze, right? Why would you need a book to tell you how to do it? Okay, so if you are already practicing mindfulness every day and reaping the rewards you can be totally smug and gift this book to one of your stressed-out friends.

But the chances are you're not already practicing mindfulness on a regular basis and you are perhaps suffering from stress, overload and the inability to see the great uniqueness in your own beautiful world. Mindfulness practice is deceptively simple – in that the steps to learn how to be mindful can be taught and with time they can become second-nature. However, just because something is simple is does not mean it is easy. Driving a car is simple once you've mastered each individual action and assimilated it into your efficient brain. But ask any teenager taking his or her first lesson: learning to drive a car is not that easy. Not at first. And nor is mindfulness. Which is why you need to practice.

Anybody can do it

Yes, they can. I can, you can, anyone can. All that is required is a willingness to take that leap of faith and begin with a simple 3 minute meditation. In fact, you've already proved that anyone can do it because you did the Day 1 Mindfulness Meditation at the beginning of this chapter. And now you've seen how simple it is, you're ready to take the next step.

WHAT MINDFULNESS ISN'T

Just before we move on to finding out all the wonderful benefits mindfulness can bring, let's just take a moment to think about what mindfulness isn't.

Mindfulness versus concentration

There is some confusion about whether mindfulness and concentration are in fact the same thing. I just sit and look at this stone, right, and concentrate on it really hard? That way all my thoughts are focused on this stone and I'm doing mindfulness. Right?

Not quite.

Although you will need to employ a certain amount of concentration during your mindfulness practice, concentration and mindfulness are very different things. Concentration is a way of forcing the mind to stay on one thing, one point. It is the word force that runs counter to mindfulness. Forcing the mind to focus on something is not the same as paying attention. Being able to concentrate will aid your mindfulness practice, but mindfulness is the act of not trying to achieve anything. Where concentration is perceived as exclusively forcing the mind and struggling to stay focused, mindfulness is stepping back and allowing the mind to observe.

To use the stone analogy once more, concentration sees only the stone, while mindfulness is aware of the stone, and aware of the effort to focus on the stone, but is also able to notice the distraction that occurs when attention is drawn away from the stone and concentration drifts. Mindfulness practice pulls the concentration gently back, without judgment or concept of 'failing' to concentrate.

Not positive thinking

Another common misconception is that mindfulness is the same as positive thinking. There is, of course, nothing wrong with positive thinking! But this is also a form of controlling, of changing what is there (negative thoughts) to another state (positive thoughts). While there is a place for this is in self-help strategies, mindfulness is about the "willingness to be with what is". If, while practicing mindfulness meditation, you find yourself trying to prop up or reinforce your efforts with positive self-talk, such as "Hey, Tamsyn, you're doing really well here. You haven't thought about work for at least two minutes now", acknowledge your thoughts without judgment and let them pass. There is more on this in the next chapter.

Not "formal" meditation

Early we talked briefly about formal meditation, and the difference between this and mindfulness. I just want to reiterate that difference, so you're completely clear. And it is tricky to be clear on the difference because the definitions of mindfulness and meditation often overlap, not least of all because when we talk about practicing mindfulness in a conscious way we use the term mindfulness meditation, or guided mindfulness meditations.

Another way of looking at it is to think of mindfulness as a type of meditation, distinct from other types, such as Buddhist, transcendental, or yoga meditation. But don't get hung up on this. Sometimes our brains try to categorize stuff as a way of controlling information, and in order to throw out ideas that don't fit within the confines of what we already know. However you want to think of mindfulness practice, whether as meditation or not, you will still get the fantastic benefits from it. Let's move on to find out exactly what they might be.

WHAT'S IN IT FOR ME?

Many studies have shown that mindfulness practice, even after only six days, can bring about a whole host of physical, psychological and social benefits. Mindfulness is great for:

Our minds! Well, you'd kind of expect this. Studies have shown that mindfulness increases positive emotions and decreases feelings of stress and anxiety. Some researchers have found that mindfulness practice is as effective as antidepressants for combating depression.

Our bodies. After eight weeks of practice, mindfulness can boost the body's immune system and help to fight off illness. Then there are the benefits of increased relaxation, reduction in occurrences of headaches and migraine, and the elimination of many aches and pains associated with tension and stress.

Our memory and mental processes. Research shows that mindfulness actually increases the density of gray matter in the brain, leading to improvements in learning and memory. And by learning to tune out distractions, mindfulness improves our attention skills, with benefits across the board at home and at work.

Our families and friends. Mindfulness helps us become more compassionate and empathetic. We become better at regulating our emotions – and therefore less likely to fly off the handle when stressed! There is also evidence to show that mindfulness improves compassion for the self, which feeds into a positive spiral. Relationships strengthen and improve when just one partner practices mindfulness: studies have shown that regular practice makes you feel more optimistic and accepting, and therefore closer to loved ones.

Parents. Many parents report feeling more in control and calmer when dealing with problems such as tantrums or teenage behaviour. Mindfulness improves parenting skills, which has a knock-on effect of improving their children's social skills and sense of self-esteem. Even parents-to-be can benefit, with research showing that mindfulness can reduce both pregnancy related anxiety and post-natal depression.

When you practice mindfulness you will find yourself in a much less stressful world that is full of vivid images, sounds, tastes, smells and experiences. You can expect improved performance at work and in the home, and a greater sense of personal contentment. Ready to find out more? Now we know the Why, let's find out more about the How To of mindfulness practice.

Chapter 2: Meditation

Meditation is perhaps the most popular technique when it comes to practicing stress reduction. It is popularly practiced by going to a quiet location and then closing one's eyes in order to be more in tune with nature. Doing this makes a person become aware of one's thoughts and enables a person to listen to his own body.

The practice of meditation goes a long way back into history – the ancients have practiced this as a form of prayer, in order for them to communicate with nature, or spiritual deities that they believe would grant them peace and good health.

Today, meditation is being practiced not only for spiritual reasons, but also for its health benefits. Since spirituality has been linked to mental health, meditation is also being practiced nowadays to achieve stress relief.

The following techniques all use meditation and are guaranteed to instantly relieve stress, no matter where you are.

1. Visualization Meditation

Visualization, also termed as guided imagery, is a form of traditional meditation that would prompt you to put your sensations into action. This classic form of meditation requires you to imagine that you are in a peaceful place, such as a beach or in the mountain.

As you imagine yourself in this calm and beautiful scenery, you begin to release your hold on feelings of anxiety.

Here are the steps on how to do this type of meditation:

Go to a quiet place where you can relax. Take note that you might fall asleep during this exercise, so you may opt to do this while sitting comfortably, yet upright in a chair.

Close your eyes and imagine your favorite type of place to relax. Picture that image as vividly as possible — if it is the beach, think about the sound of the waves or the feel of the sand on your feet. Think about how the air smells, if there are birds or other natural sounds.

Explore the area within your mind, until the picture becomes more vivid as if you are actually experiencing it. Imagine that you are building sand castles or riding a fisherman's boat. Feel the waves splashing on your as you lie in the beach close to the water.

If you think that your mind wanders from one spot to another during this exercise, do not worry about it – it is a normal response. It is also normal that you would feel stiffness in your limbs or a tingling sensation.

2. Mantra Meditation

Mantra meditation is a form of relaxation wherein you repeat a soothing word over and over again so that your body can relax. This traditional Buddhist mindfulness exercise is in fact composed of two stages – the mantra, and the meditation itself. It is commonly practiced as a form of prayer. Here is how you can do it.

Sit in a quiet and relaxing spot, preferably right after you wake up. Close your eyes.

Pay attention to your body, while feeling the environment around you. Breathe deeply in a slow rhythm. Relax.

Say your chosen mantra, making sure that the sound resonates through your chest.

Imagine that the words you are chanting echoes through your body.

The mantras that you should choose can be anything, as long as they represent the reality that you want to embody. Keep in mind that mantras are traditionally used to represent one's relationship with the gods or nature. But could be as simple as remembering a feeling you want to have, such as peace, relaxed, or calm.

Here are some common mantras you can use:

Om Mani Padme Hum – (Oh-m Mahnee Podmee Hum) means "Hail the Jewel in the Lotus," and is used to pay respect to the Buddha of Compassion

I am that I am – this mantra came from the Torah, which represents how God introduced himself to Moses

Ham-Sah – this is the Hindu variant oh I am that I am

Aum – or Om, a sacred sound with Hindu origins that means To Become, Will Be, or It Is.

Namo AmitaBha – mantra used to pay respect to Buddha's immortal light

You can also use modern mantras such as "I change my thoughts, I change my world," or "Be the change you wish to see in the world."

The number of times that you chant a mantra can be dictated through the use of the mala beads, which can have 108 or 21 beads, which has a mystical meaning in Hinduism. However, you can choose to chant your mantra as many times as you deem fitting.

3. Meditation Walking

Meditation walking is practically one of the easiest and most practical ways of finding peace of mind. For most people, this can take the form of a leisurely walk, with them just paying attention to everything that they see around them.

When you take a meditative walk, you feel that your body and mind experience togetherness, and become fully aware that you are living in the present. You feel how your feet feel as they meet and leave the earth with each step, the sounds around you, the smells and feelings of a breeze or calm air surrounding you.

The wonderful thing about this technique is that you can do this every time you need to go out. Take the time to give your car or the public transportation a break – simply walk from Point A to Point B without hurrying and focus on your environment. That simple leisurely walk that you can do every day can bring you a good break from stress.

4. Mindful Breathing

This is also one of the most popular MBSR techniques that can be very handy to learn, since you can do this regardless of the location or situation you are. This brings to mind the most important body activity that reminds you that you exist and that you live – breathing.

To do this, all you need to do is to pay attention on every breath you take in and out, and calm your mind while you do so. Without much effort, you would feel that your mind and sensations are beginning to become much clearer.

After these mentioned techniques, you may want to proceed to giving focus on your physiology and find out which parts of your body in particular experience physical stress. The next chapter would be all about relaxing your body by focusing on areas that are normally affected by tension.

Chapter 3: Benefits of Mindfulness

Mindfulness is a tool that is meant to empower individuals. It helps in letting the practitioner experience life as they live it. It gives the necessary pause needed in dealing with emotional issues or mental anguish. It also helps us understand how our mind and emotions work, in which we will be able to use that knowledge to direct our lives.

To further show you the power of mindfulness, here are some of the benefits in the different aspect of our lives:

Mindfulness helps us be more "receptive" than "reactive" - It gives you the chance to detach and observe your thoughts and emotions and not just be overpowered by it. It will help you dictate your words, reactions and behaviors; practicing mindfulness will act as a mental regulator.

For example, you are now more aware of what is really happening in a certain situation, even before that situation leads to a worse scenario, you can easily deal with it. Even if it seems like a habitual path for you, you can now pause and choose your reaction well. In short, it changes how you react to the symptoms and not necessarily the symptoms itself.

Mindfulness is often used for therapies especially in treating depression - One of the programs used is Mindfulness-Based Cognitive Therapy. According to studies, depression, anxiety, stress and even irritability will all decrease as you practice this. You are more likely to associate and recognize the positive things than to dwell with psychological distress as it helps you understand and deal with your emotion. Even the US Marine troops have undergone mindfulness meditation training, and not only did it improve their performances, but also helped them in handling stress. In addition, mindfulness can literally lower the stress hormone cortisol. In turn, your happiness level is increased.

Mindfulness reveals our true selves - oftentimes when you view ourselves, we have certain biases or preformed perception. The practice of mindfulness, however, promotes on looking things objectively and as if the rose-colored glasses is lifted. By doing so, not only are we able to fill in the "blind spots" but we also now have a better understanding of ourselves and of others. Why? In the process, we become familiar with our thought patterns. It then teaches us about our traits (not only the obvious ones) and what makes us really tick. For example, as you begin to be aware of yourself, you start to recognize these thoughts that can lead to depression, stress or anxiety. With mindfulness, you can now catch yourself even before the thoughts can lead to destruction.

Mindfulness gives us peace of mind with less negative thoughts and emotions - this is one of the aspects of practicing mindfulness that I love. It disempowers the negative thoughts that we have. How? Our negative thoughts or even emotions will continue to build up when we "nurture" it and continue to focus on it. But will mindfulness, yes, you recognize your thoughts and emotions, and even observe your reactions, but they key here is that you now look at it without passing judgment or look at it uncritically.

For example, when you are very angry at someone, you want to start breaking things and say hurtful things to relieve yourself of the heavy emotion. But with mindfulness, your train of thoughts will be, "Yes I am angry at the moment, I recognize what triggers it, but I don't want this anger to manifest. I don't need to do any drastic move because I also know that this emotion will pass." You may even start employing some breathing control, and you will start to feel the strong and dark emotion starting to subside.

Mindfulness actually strengthens the immune system and even our physiological responses against negative emotions or feelings such as stress.

The practice of mindfulness can actually help an individual be more open to other people, new experiences and reduced negative associations.

Mindfulness is good for your health - According to studies, aside from strengthening the immune system, it can also help promote chromosomal health and resilience. In effect, it can reduce signs of ageing at a cellular level. Mindfulness could also help control blood sugar, improve the circulatory health, and reduce risk of diseases and hypertension as it helps regulate blood pressure. Another health-related benefit is that it also helps alleviate chronic pain symptoms.

Mindfulness can improve your cognitive function, mental resilience and working memory - this practice can also enhance your creativity as you are more in touch with yourself and your surroundings. Students can really benefit from utilizing mindfulness techniques.

Mindfulness can dramatically reduce distractions and improve your focus - Of course, this is one of the very essences of mindfulness, and that is being able to eliminate the "noise" and focus more, thus we become more alert and will achieve mental balance. I would like to stress that with mindfulness, you intend to live your life moment by moment minus the distractions. You do not "escape", but begin to recognize what needs to be done and changed, which will be your focus.

You will begin to see the bigger picture by being mindful -Using the same example that I have given earlier: you are at the peak of your anger, you want to lash out, scream hurtful things and even be physical to express your anger, but when you practice mindfulness, you will have that necessary pause, and think, "Is the reason why I'm angry worth the possible destruction of our relationship? Is s/he entirely at fault? What are the possible consequences of my actions? Will I let anger define me? In a few hours or days, will my reaction still be the same?"

As you also start to calm yourself, and achieve clarity, you will now begin to see possible solutions or how you can deal with the situation. You will also begin to understand what truly matters.

Develop deeper wisdom and connection through mindfulness - As the noise dies down, as you intently observe and listen to things, your wisdom will also be developed since your way of thinking is not only caged in a particular pattern. You begin to look at yourself, others and the situation in a different light. You feel strong connections, may it be with an inanimate object or another person. As you begin to notice and feel things with your senses, a deeper sense of gratitude and understanding will also follow. You will develop a sense of intimacy, and things will feel much more alive as you live through each moment. It might sound a bit of "romantic" but think of it as being able to bridge any gap, developing a new eye in looking at things, and noticing every detail, which will also add more purpose and meaning into our lives.

If you feel a bit of empty, maybe mindlessness is one of the reasons why. Because of it, you did not live with every moment and the things that you are looking or yearning for are actually just within the reach all along, if only you have noticed.

With mindfulness, you become a more compassionate and loving person as you begin to understand and have connections with the people that surrounds you - You also become less critical, judgmental and combative; instead you learn how to embrace the situation and each person's individuality and vulnerability.

You have now read some of the wonderful effects of mindfulness. But I also have to give a word of caution before you start. If you practice mindfulness for a specific purpose, like to help you relax or reduce negative tensions, there is a change that it won't work. Why? We should focus less on the possible outcomes or "side effect" and focus more on just living the moment. The desire for that particular effect can overpower the real purpose of mindfulness. For example, instead of relaxing (the desired outcome), since you are actively thinking about it, and the more that you think about relaxing, the more that you will tense up (especially if you suddenly feel that it is taking too long). So take my word, embrace the suggested exercises for mindfulness, live in the moment, forget the outcome, and in the end you will be surprised how far you have come.

Chapter 4: The 8 Attitudes That Defines a Mindful Heart.

As a beginner in mindfulness practice, you may be thinking that being mindful is a difficult step to take, but in actual sense, it is not. Even if you are unsure about how to proceed, you can start by learning about the attitudes that will define a mindful heart.

Just before mindfulness practices, it is important to know the concept behind mindfulness and what it means to be a mindful person especially when you are making extra efforts toward personal growth. The eight attitudes that that will contribute towards a flourishing mind, and personal growth are;

#1: A curious mind- You need to see things as a visitor, in a foreign land, this means you are curious about all beliefs and why an unpleasant situation has stuck to your mind. You need to see each situation as new and you are willing to investigate the situation to know if it is good for you to embrace or discard.

#2: A Non-judgmental mind- a mindful person is impartial, and doesn't label a person or situation as good or bad, right or wrong until they have completed their own investigation and thoroughly understand the person, situation or things. A mindful person will simply allow a situation to be.

#3: Acknowledges – a mindful person will recognize things as they are.

#4: Settled heart- A mindful person is comfortable in the moment and has contentment.

#5: Composure- A mindful person is composed, he or she remains in control with great insight and compassion.

#6: He lets things be- A mindful person does not feel the need to change everything. He lets things be with no need to force things to change in his or her favor.

#7: He is self-reliant – He makes decisions based on his or her own experiences and understanding. He or she knows what is true and what is not, hence he makes a decision based on thorough investigation of situations.

#8: He is self-compassionate – a mindful person does not indulge in self-reproach, he loves himself as he is with no criticism.

Now that you are aware of the attitude of a mindful person, these are the attitudes you must endeavor to cultivate because they form the basis of living in the moment and acquiring the power of Now!

As a mindful person the way you react to a situation must be positive, those who react negatively to situations often find themselves enmeshed in bigger problems that can break them and make them lose total control. If you can develop the highlighted mindful attitudes above, your life and lives of the people around you will be better off.

What are the attitudes that will aid your Mindfulness practices?

If you want to be successful, you need to allow it to happen, which means, your entire being must be brought into the techniques. Your attitude towards mindfulness techniques is very essential it is simply the "fertile soil" where you want to cultivate that power of Now! That is, the ability to bring your mind to calmness, relaxation, and improve your capabilities to see more clearly. The following attitudes have been found to increase your success rates in mindfulness practices;

The beginner's mind,

Patience,

Persistence,

Non-striving,

Self-assurance or self-trust,

Letting-it-go, and

Acceptance.

#1: The Beginner's mind- This attitude is the one in which you believe a situation is new, even if you are familiar with it. For instance, "I have been enjoying this crunchy cereal mix for a while, maybe the taste will be different today". Having a beginner's mind is very important because it can help you get that freshness of breath over and over again. It is an attitude that raises your optimism and help you approach a situation more effectively.

#2: Patience- Patience is one of the fruits of wisdom, it is the ability to resist the urge to rush through the moment and remain opened to each moment as they come by. When you are open to a new moment, you will explore its fullness and seize every opportunity that comes with it. When you are opened to the moment, you will completely believe that things will eventually un-fold with time. You may be thinking that your body's clock is ticking away, being patient means you will avoid errors that will lead you nowhere.

#3: Just like patience, persistence is another attitude that can greatly help you to become mindful of your thoughts and actions. When you are patient even through the darkest of times, you have the believe that the steps you take everyday will eventually bring you to the desired end you wished for yourself. Persistence simply means "to keep on going". Even if you have little benefits coming in, you need to stick to your practice of mindfulness because there will always be a big break and new discoveries in being persistent.

#4: Non-striving – striving is the process of struggling or trying too hard to achieve something, which is a complete opposite of non-striving. Humans do strive in different ways, we want to please others by looking like them, we strive to become more relaxed, and we even strive too hard to make more money. It is important to remember while we are striving that the only thing we should do is to become mindful of the results we are getting, and then return to the main focus of our ambition or practice especially when we fail and realized that we have been distracted.

When you accept things as they are, you wouldn't strive too hard to please yourself or anyone else, you will become mindful and trust yourself more, while honoring your feelings.

#5: Acceptance is an attitude that can be described as the willingness to "let go". Acceptance does not mean you must settle for your current condition, neither does it mean you must accept injustice being meted to you. Acceptance simply means, you have come to understand why a situation is like that

How to deal with the hindrances to mindfulness practices

Perhaps the best possible way to do away with all hindrances to mindful practices is to set out a regular mindfulness practice. You may want to start your mindfulness practices before your evening meals or just before you go for shower. Just make sure you stick to the schedule and to make it easier, you need to make use of the same place. Many people may think there are no clear ways of preventing old harmful thoughts from coming back, but in actual sense, they are the ones who are not willing to replace those thoughts with present realities.

The biggest obstacle to mindfulness perhaps, is having an idea of the right way to go about the mindful practices. Mindfulness techniques should make you feel more relaxed especially when you were initially stressed. When you are still feeling agitated during and after your mindfulness exercises, then you are probably doing it the wrong way.

That state of calmness remains one of the main benefits of mindfulness, it is important to note that we need to put our general mood into perspectives in order to be certain whether we have achieved calmness or not. You have not attained calmness when you feel relaxed but your old beliefs and thoughts are still in control.

Finding time for mindfulness exercises is another obstacle. Most people say they are too busy to find the time to practice meditation. When you are curious about mindfulness, you will definitely find time to indulge in its practice. You need to be clear about the steps to be taken during mindful practices, then you can slot in even few minutes a day to indulge in the exercises. Another option is to indulge in mindful practices at the end of the day when you are about to retire into your bed.

Chapter 5: Powerful Steps to Self-Love

Most of us have grown up thinking that we need others to love who we are so that we can be happy. Wanting others to love you is no bad goal. However, if you're going to stop at nothing in order to be loved, if you're going to let others have their way at your expense, then that's unfair to yourself. Self-love is treating yourself as you would a good friend. It is about satisfying your needs and forgiving yourself. Self-love is associated with the following:

Low anxiety

Low depression

More happiness

More optimism

Healthy habits

The following are some of the practices that boost self-love.

Start your day on a positive note

Start your day by telling yourself something that will put a smile on your face. When you hit your day off on a positive note, you get to take on other activities of the day with a positive mindset. You can start the day by reminding yourself of how well you handled a situation, the important role that you play in someone's life or in a company, and so on.

Eat healthy foods

Research has shown that there's a correlation between the foods we eat and our emotional state. If we eat unhealthy foods like junk, we are more likely to be stressed out and anxious than if we eat a meal consisting of nutritious ingredients. Food is our fuel. For the optimal functioning of our body, we need to consume foods that will nourish us and provide us with the energy to complete various tasks. Healthy meals encourage us to cook our meals at home instead of eating out, thus saving money.

Workout

The more fit you are, the more likely you are to experience happy feelings and have high self-esteem. But if your body is in a terrible shape, you are likely to suffer low self-esteem and it will contribute to making poor decisions. Get into the habit of working out regularly. The following are some of the benefits associated with exercising.

improved heart health

improved blood circulation

improved brain health

improved sleep quality

improved moods

There are various ways, both expensive and inexpensive to get started on working out.

Silence your inner critic

There's an inner critic inside each one of us that complicates things. This critic is harsh on us and makes us feel terrible. We should make a point of silencing this critic before they bring us major harm. But this doesn't mean we should ignore any form of criticism.

Surround yourself with positive people

They say that a person is the average of the five people they spend the most time with. True. Make a point of spending time with only positive individuals. This will make you take on their positive traits and help you become better at making decisions.

Stop comparing yourself with others

There will always be people more successful and less successful than you. But more importantly, success can adhere to your own definition. Have your own idea of success. Comparing yourself to other people will take away your self-worth when you come up short.

Cut off toxic people

Toxic people are nothing more than energy vampires. They will steal away your positive energy and leave you feeling terrible. Make a point of getting rid of them. Of course, it is not easy to distance yourself from toxic people especially if you have been the energy supply but take baby steps first like refusing to hang out with them and then large steps like changing residence.

Celebrate your wins

There's nothing like "a small win". If you make a step forward, always get into a celebratory mood. Being grateful to yourself will allow you to tap into the whole of your potential. Winning in small ways will instill a winning mindset into your subconscious and you are far more likely to achieve most of your goals.

Step out of your comfort zone

As long as you're in your comfort zone, you will never know what you're really capable of. Push yourself out of your comfort zone and watch your life turn around. Success is always found in the extra effort that we apply. If you are looking for a life partner, try to meet more people instead of locking yourself away and complaining that there are no suitable partners.

Embrace your quirkiness

If you have some traits that are considered "out of the norm", you should embrace them instead of being ashamed of them. If you stand tall with your quirkiness, you will draw people in. There will be a sense of uniqueness about you.

Follow your passion

It's the one thing that excites you but at the same time, you're scared of failing. Overcome your fear of failure and go for your passion. Many successful people have revealed that their secret to success is merely following what they are most passionate about.

Help others

By helping others, we get a huge sense of fulfillment. It is incredibly satisfying to lighten the burden of other people. It is also a form of networking. Life is interconnected. At one point, you may require something and find yourself needing the expertise of the person that you helped in which case it will be rendered easily.

Strengthen your relationships

You're not resourceful enough to stay on your own. You will always depend on others, particularly your life partner. Work on strengthening your close relationships so that you can enjoy abundant peace of mind and support.

Give up the need for approval of others

No matter what you do, there will always be someone to find fault with it. Desist from trying to be in everyone's good book. Think about it, when everyone likes you, you won't have anyone to prove yourself to and your success will be kind of bland. You know why Sylvester Stallone feels so great about himself? It's because he received a lot of rejection before he finally got his breakthrough. And now he feels great knowing that all those executives that shunned him have helplessly seen him become a star.

CHAPTER 6: CALM THE MIND

Learning how to calm the mind is one of the most essential steps of learning meditation. Each of us has what looks like millions of voices that echo every day through our heads. Some of these voices are positive, some are negative, and some of them sound like a four-year-old gaggle on a high sugar. The following is a guide to help you learn how to calm your mind to start a meditation session.

The first step is to believe your mind can be quiet. Many of us agree that even for a single second it would be difficult to silence their minds. We never will, as long as they believe they can't. They will subconsciously work every time to undermine their efforts. So believe it is possible and as you continue with the following exercise reinforce that you believe with every voice that quiets, but make sure that you do not produce other voices celebrating what others have quieted.

First, begin by sitting in a quiet room, preferably a chair, somewhere comfortable. Close your eyes and listen to the sound in your mind without judgment. Hearing may take a few seconds, but you're going to start hearing voices speaking, singing, or even repeating random noises quickly. Listen. These are the voices that always talk, twenty-four hours a day, while you start your day. Now, choose one of the cacophony voices.

Recognize it, hear or sing what it has to say. Then give her closure by turning her volume down slowly until she can't be heard. Don't miss it! The echo will just keep repeating whether or not you pay attention to it. For each speech, continue this process. Some voices you ignored might come back, not get angry or frustrated, accept and then reject it.

This practice may need to be performed on a daily basis for days, weeks, or even months at a time in some extreme cases. Don't be disappointed about your success. Each journey takes as many times as it needs. Alternatively, reflect on the gains you've made and use it to strengthen your commitment to learn how to meditate.

Many have succeeded in calming the mind even though others have struggled. The discrepancies between success and failure can often be seen in the approach to the mission that you carry out. Here are three tips to help you as a successful person to be among the winners. Follow the following tips and you can be confident that the results will be good!

Next, in a place where you won't be interrupted, you want to go and relax. You need to stop the distraction and do this the right way. If you do this, you'll help to calm your mind completely, you'll end up in good shape. If you neglect it or fail to pay attention to it, you may face the same problems with which you started. If you do it wrong by trying to calm your mind in a busy atmosphere, then you may be faced with a task to relax your mind, which is the overall goal here. Second, you can close your eyes and sit in silence for 15 minutes. It is important for these reasons: sitting in silence results in the mind relaxing completely without effort failing to do this is likely to mean that you struggle to calm the body when you eventually fail to calm the mind second, you have to try to do this only at a time when you feel overwhelmed. Ignore them and it's just not a good prediction. It's up to you to adopt them and reap the benefits; ignore them and you probably won't. Failure to follow these tips and relax the mind will almost certainly remain a far-off sight...

Meditation Methods to Relax the Mind

If you're looking to learn one of the many common meditation techniques to relax your mind. Every one of them is nice not only to calm you down but also to concentrate your mind. For time to time, all of us have some pressures for which we need relief. If you also suffer from these stresses, then you will learn to meditate. There are so many different techniques to choose from that you'll find one that suits you.

Meditation is the art of making constructive thoughts and feelings into your negative stresses. You have to calm down to meditate, and you also have to be careful because sometimes it's hard to focus your mind in a positive direction.

This is particularly true if you face more tension than normal. But you can change the focus of your mind with the right amount of wisdom and help calm your body in the process.

You will cure your troubled mind through meditation. It helps you to think more clearly and prevent other diseases that may arise when your life is overtaken by stress. To cure other mental disorders, you can even meditate.

Understanding the techniques of meditation can help with attacks of depression, anxiety and panic. You just meditate on a more positive frame of mind instead of going down these roads. However, this will most definitely take some practice. The more you are suffering from these illnesses, the more you are used to a pessimistic way of thinking. Under these conditions, it may take you a little longer to reach the meditative state, but once you do, you can understand how important it can be to help overcome these disorders.

A very effective form of meditation uses a mantra as a soothing process. While you sit with your eyes shut repeating the mantra or tone, you practice 15 to 20 minutes a day.

From a number of gurus or master practitioners, you will learn different types of meditation. You can then compare the various techniques to see which one or more of them will give you the best results. You should try lessons on DVDs, videos or recordings if you don't have any classes at your fingertips. You can get a teacher to train you properly in this way.

After a while, you may not need the classes or the videos when you know what you're doing. Our mental state is dramatically linked to our physical state, so it can also cause physical problems if it is adversely affected. Using meditation in periods of emotional distress or trauma to relax your mind may help to minimize the negative impact that the experience may have on your body.

Whether you're learning your meditation from a video, a guru, or an online practitioner, today you need to look into it. Through managing stress more productively, you'll learn to feel more peace and harmony in your life.

Calm the Mind with Exercise

There are also certain mental benefits that come along with the physical, along with the obvious physical benefits associated with exercise. A great motivator for exercise can be the connection between mental health and fitness.

One of the main advantages of exercise is that you are both more productive and creative when you are in good health and physically fit. It can also increase your trust and make your days so much easier, especially if you need to keep up with your kids or co-workers.

A series of emotional benefits offered by exercise are as follows:

1. Exercise will ease your mind and help you to relax at work and home.

2. Exercise can strengthen the relationship between body and mind, as well as reduce the symptoms of certain ailments and illnesses such as common cold, gastrointestinal disorders, arthritis, and even cancer.

3. Exercise can enhance memory retention and help you stay on your feet. This will reduce the risk of Alzheimer's disease and other forms of dementia.

4. Exercise can help increase bone density, making osteoporosis and stress fractures less likely to occur.

5. Exercise can improve confidence, which can also have a positive impact on your health, social and professional life.

6. Exercise will make you more comfortable. Many people who exercise regularly are happier and more confident than people who are mostly sedentary.

7. Exercise allows you the time to consider things, circumstances, and life. Lots of tension can be worked out.

8. Exercise can make you feel better about yourself as well. You'll feel healthier and look healthier, making you more desirable to others. It includes colleagues as well as forward-looking dates.

9. Exercise will teach your children the value of exercise. By training, you can be a great role model.

10. Exercise may reduce any anxiety and depression feelings. Through regular physical activity, both depression and anxiety can be minimized.

11. That's right. Exercise helps in a more positive light to convey frustrations, indignation, negative energy, as well as disappointments. Both physically and psychologically, in order to improve familiar and pleasant relationships, exercise can provide the person with more confidence and energy.

Aerobics and other types of exercise can be a great way to get yourself inspired and boost your emotional state. It has the potential to help your soul, body, and mind if you can stay focused on exercise.

Chapter 7: Meditation Tips and Techniques

Below are a collection of mindfulness techniques that you may want to try, either all of them or just some of them. You may develop your own mindfulness technique that works best for you.

But here are some suggestions that might interest you to try:

1. Place a photograph of a calm nature shot near your computer. Look at it with relaxed intention every now and then.

2. Put a plant on your desk in a pot and look at t once in a while with relaxed intention.

3. Close your eyes and give relaxed attention to the sensations in your feet.

4. Fill a plastic water bottle one third of the way with water, and put the lid on it. Close your eyes and give relaxed attention to the sound of the water in the bottle as you turn the bottle with your hands.

5. Give relaxed attention to your chest or abdomen.

6. Give relaxed attention to what you read.

7. While doing laundry give relaxed attention to your hands as you work. The slower you work the easier it is.

8. Mindfully shower and give relaxed attention to the soap against your skin.

9. Give relaxed attention on what it feels like to be angry, happy, sad, irritated, stressed out, or frustrated.

10. Give relaxed attention to you body when you feel stressed out.

11. When you go for a walk, pay attention to the movements of your feet. The Slower you walk the easier it is.

12. Give relaxed attention to the smell of freshly brewed coffee or baked bread.

13. Give relaxed attention to the sun, moon, clouds, and stars.

14. Listen mindfully to the sound of rain or other sounds of nature like thunder.

15. Sit next to a waterfall and give relaxed attention to the sounds or vibrations you feel.

16. Give relaxed attention to wind against your skin

17. Go to the beach and take in the smell, what do the waves sound like? Only give relaxed attention to one meditation object at a time.

18. Listen to music or watch a movie mindfully. Giving relaxed attention to what you hear and see.

19. Listen mindfully to great meditation talks by great masters.

20. Give relaxed attention to the souls of your feet.

All you have to do is give relaxed attention to your meditation object. Relax and enjoy the present moment.

Chapter 8: Be Mindful Everyday

The previous chapter helped you by giving you steps on how you are going to become more mindful. Now, this chapter will give you tips on how you can do small things in your everyday life that will lead you to become more mindful too. After all, small things can pile up into bigger things. Here are some of the things you can try.

Start your day with mindfulness

The moment you open your eyes, start your day right by being mindful. Do not just wake up and rush your way through your daily routine. Instead, appreciate each of the steps that compose your morning starting from the alarm clock that wakes you up each day. Look outside your window and look at the sunrise that you might have probably overlooked each passing morning. Then appreciate the beauty of nature and be thankful that today, you are still alive.

Let your mind wander

You have to let your mind have some time of its own and let it explore the world before it. When you do, you think of thoughts you have not thought of before and it helps you to look at the world differently, to see people in a different light. In a way, it helps you make non-bias decisions and it can also help you to stop being judgemental and such. So why not practice letting your mind wander today?

All you need to do is just let your mind take you where it wants to.

Make it short

You should not be stuck on being mindful throughout your day. Stick to at least 20 minutes of mindfulness then go back to your original thoughts because the mind is more susceptible to short lengths of mindfulness. Just like the attention span, it is better to keep it short so that it sticks in your mind better.

Reverse the order of things

This should be fun especially if you are the type of person that is very uptight. Forget about your schedule for the day and try doing things in reverse. For example, if you tend to eat before taking a shower, how about doing the opposite? Just mix things up so that you would have some refreshment in your life. Or arrange the stacks of books alphabetically but in the reverse order, from Z to A. There are many fun ways to reverse the order of things. It will help you focus and find room to forget the worries and just think about what you are doing.

Practice while you wait

You are going to be waiting somewhere within your day, maybe because of traffic or maybe in the line at the grocery store or something else. But the point is during the moment that you are waiting in line or in your car, do something better than getting your phone out of your pocket and trying to busy yourself with it. Instead, try to practice being mindful while you are waiting. Look at the people around you, and try to make an analysis of them, try to understand the things they are doing and why they might be doing it. These simple things will help you become a whole lot more mindful.

Write with the opposite hand

It would be challenging at first but being ambidextrous can be practiced. For a day or a week, try doing things with your weak hand. If you are right handed, why not try writing with your left hand first and then move on to things that might be a bit more advanced like holding your spoon and fork in the opposite hands. Just remember to be more cautious and careful when you are trying this out so that you do not hurt yourself in the process.

Pick a reminder

Because your brain can only handle so much, it is good to get a reminder to tell you when you should start being mindful again. For example, you can try picking a certain door or pen or something that you do not usually use, then make that as a reminder, as if whenever you see that item, you begin to change into a mindful mode.

Change your routine

Stop your habits! Give it a break and try something new today, take a different route, talk to a different person and just change your daily routine. Make it more exciting. Order that coffee you've been avoiding all week or that donut that you think might give you extra calories. Run that mile you thought you could not and prove to people that you can do things when you've put your mind into it. Do things that might mess up with your routine but would definitely make you happy.

Surfing through your urges

There are moments when you have certain urges or cravings and you are not sure on what action you will take to get through them. Now, you need to take this as a wake-up call to be mindful. You need not do anything about them, you need not go and fight it or answer to your cravings. Just try to understand the reason why you feel that way and be mindful of that.

Stop and smile

When things get so hard for you at work, just stop everything you are doing and smile for a while. It may not seem that helpful but when you smile, your brain secretes hormones that eventually makes you feel happy. So remember to just smile no matter what you may be going through because not only will it cause people who look at you to smile as well but you are also helping yourself to become happier.

Pick simple objects

In order to become more mindful, just take it easy and start small. Pick up simple objects to concentrate on and just stare at it for 5 minutes or so. Then think of all the things that may be happening to the object right now if you have not picked it up and the other millions of possibilities that could happen to it once you dropped it down. Be aware of the universe and the way it works. Think about yourself, a dot to the millions of stars in the universe but a dot that can someday make a difference in the world that you are living in.

Sit often

When you sit, your mind becomes more susceptible to observations and thinking, so try to sit down more often and let your senses become aware of your surroundings. This is also one way to be mindful of your environment, to be able to sit anywhere and focus your mind on what you want to focus on.

Put phone in airplane mode

Whenever you are going to be somewhere important like meetings, seminars and things like that, you need to keep your phone in airplane mode so that your thoughts would not be disturbed. This makes you a more mindful listener and helps you to be a better person. This also reduces the time you spend looking at your phone. If you try to do this daily or at least for some certain length of time during each day, you will see a big improvement in your mindfulness.

Be patient

It may take a bit of your time to focus and practice especially when you are just starting to be mindful. But do not fear, you will eventually get there as long as you put your very best into it. Be patient and know that good things come to those who know how to handle themselves in tough situations.

Do not accept excuses

When you find yourself telling you that you are just not meant to be mindful, stop yourself. Do not accept any excuses that you are bound to tell yourself to stop you from being mindful. It is not acceptable because you can actually be mindful if you just keep on practicing. You are bound to eventually get better so just be on your toes and keep your best foot forward.

Have fun

Do not be so serious! Enjoy what you are doing and be passionate about it. That way, you would not even notice time flying by. You ought to have fun in these activities so that you will be able to be happy while being mindful at the same time. Relax and just do your very best. It will all work out fine in the end so do not worry too much and just go with the flow.

Now you have learned steps on how you are going to be more mindful by doing simple steps on each passing day. You are bound to be more mindful once you have done these steps enough and if you continue on doing them every single day from this moment onwards. The next chapter will help you to find the common mistakes and misunderstandings about mindfulness so that you would be able to know how you are going to deal with it.

Chapter 9: Mindful Thoughts: You Really Need To Slow Down

If there is something mindfulness helps you do is it slows you down and makes you take life easy.

Sometimes we get so busy that we stay on the fast lane trying to keep things working and make ends meet. Does our fast-paced life help us achieve all we dream of achieving? No, it does not. While it is good to be up and doing things to make your dreams come true, a busy life without order will always end in chaos and leave you more frustrated than fulfilled. This is why your thoughts deserve as much attention as they can get.

It is actually very possible for you to become mindful of the thoughts running through your mind. One reason why you have not been able to be mindful of your thoughts is that you have never paid them any serious attention. If you pay enough attention to what you think most of the day, it will shock you to discover that most of your thoughts are unhealthy thoughts you should stop in their tracks.

A good grip of your thoughts will help you think less about things that happened in a past you cannot change and the fears you have about a future you cannot control.

You can actually stop the never-ending chatter in your head—and you must stop it—before you can succeed at noticing and being more mindful of the things happening around you and in other areas of your life. Although this will not happen automatically, with the right practices and effort, you can, at the very least, slow down your thoughts and get things under control.

To master the art of watching your thoughts intently enough to censor them, you need to master the art of mindful meditation. Mastering mindful meditation is not a case of building an overnight new habit. At first, it will look like you might never come to that point where you can sit still and think about nothing more than your breaths and change your thoughts, but consistency makes it possible.

How to Practice Mindful Meditation

These steps will help you master mindful meditation:

Before you meditate, listen to the chatter in your head and write down whatever thought crosses your mind. Most times, you will discover more than 80% of these thoughts tilt towards the negative side of life.

Write down the things you would love to think about more; you can make some sketchy descriptions—the relationship you want, the marriage you want, the job you desire, the financial status you want, the kind of neighborhood you wish to live in, etc.

Stop whatever you are doing and go somewhere serene and private, somewhere you can be alone with your thoughts

Turn off every digital gadget and other possible sources of noise such as your TV, PC, Radio, etc.

First, relax in any position of choice. You can sit or lie on your back depending on what you find comfortable.

Keep your eyes shut to keep out visual distractions

Begin with your breaths. The easiest way to begin your mastery of mindful meditation is to become mindful of your breaths

Take some deep breaths and acknowledge how they help your nerves and muscles calm down

As you begin to relax, acknowledge random thoughts non-judgmentally and return to your breaths.

As everything begins to get quiet in your head, picture the list of beautiful things you wish to see happen in your life and the kind of life you desire

Visualize these things until they become your daily realities. See yourself with that perfect partner you have always wanted. See yourself cruising around town in that Mercedes G-wagon or any exotic car of your dreams. See yourself living in your dream house. See yourself occupying that job or political position—you can visualize anything, and while at it, paint beautiful pictures and engage people in discussions in your imaginary world of possibilities.

The more you practice this, the healthier your thoughts become and drive you towards generating ideas or working harder to make these beautiful dreams come true sooner rather than later.

Mindfulness Meditation Applied in Everyday Life

As you practice mindfulness meditation and become more mindful, you can start translating your mindfulness to everything that makes you engage in negative thinking such as the places you visit, the friends you keep, and the lifestyles you engage in.

Let us see some examples:

Become more mindful of your associations

The quality of friends you keep affects the quality of your discussions, thoughts, and mind. Whatever forms the core of the discussions among your circle of friends whenever you hang out with them will always play out in your head later. Next time you are out with any friend or a group of friends, pay more attention to what they say, what they do, the things they crave, their body language, and general attitude to others and life generally. You will begin to find the ones who are always talking about the negative sides of life.

If they always have some reasons to be angry with themselves, you, or the world in general, their anger, and other such negative tendencies will always rub off on you. If they are the positive, enthusiastic type of people who seek the good in others and choose to think and talk about the beautiful things of life, their optimism, positivity and enthusiasm will also rub off on you. Spend more time with such positive friends and find some new ones if the ones you have been hanging out with have no trace of positivity or optimism in them.

Be mindful of the environment

You could be working in a toxic work environment without knowing what makes such work environment toxic. With your newfound mindfulness, you can pay more attention and thus know why you always have a sour taste in your mouth at the end of your work.

Pay attention to your job routines and your approach to tasks. Pay attention to how your superiors give out instructions to you and others. Pay attention to your colleagues and notice if they help make your job easier or more difficult. Pay attention to the orderliness of the surroundings or lack thereof.

Chances are that you may have been taking up more tasks than you can handle at any time and that has always left you mentally clouded and dissatisfied with the job when you fail to get things done well or on time.

Probably your colleagues and superiors have not been supportive and you have always allowed their negative attitudes to get to you.

Perhaps your office space is full of clutter with lots of useless files and haphazardly arranged office equipment.

The thing to do here is to change the things you can change or change the way you react to things you have no control over. You can become more organized and do things one at a time. In addition, let your colleagues or superiors know how you feel about how they relate to you and how it affects the job. You should also make an effort to avoid negative colleagues as much as you can and eliminate the clutter around you and keep things more organized to clear the fog they create in your head.

Let us now look at how you can become more mindful of your body.

Chapter 10: Being Mindful of Your Thoughts

One of the major reasons you overthink all the time (you think too much about the past or the future) is because you are not mindful of your thoughts. This means you are not aware of your thoughts. You don't know when and why a disturbing thought comes to your mind and how it affects your peace of mind, thus you don't know when and how to stop thinking on that particular thought so you can live your life in peace.

When you are mindful of your thoughts, you know when a disturbing thought comes to your mind, why it makes you feel disturbed, which disturbing memory it triggers and brings to your conscious mind and how you can stop wasting your energy on that thought as it's meaningless to hang on to it. This helps you eliminate thoughts that disturb your peace of mind and slowly increase your inner peace.

Here's how you can achieve this goal.

How to Be Mindful of Your Thoughts

To become mindful of your thoughts, you have to bring your attention to them and find out why certain thoughts disturb you. Here is a practice that you can do on a daily basis to become mindful of your thoughts.

-Pay Attention to Your Thoughts

Give yourself 5 minutes each day to make yourself aware of what's going on in your mind. Sit alone in a quiet place, close your eyes and take deep breaths.

While you take deep breaths, bring your attention to your thoughts. Observe the ones that enter your conscious mind. Is it an experience from your past that's coming over and over again into your mind or is it something in the future that is bothering you as you are not able to let go of the worry?

-Don't Indulge in Your Thoughts

While you pay attention to your thoughts, you may find that there are some that you are holding on to since you keep thinking about them recurrently and as you do that, you feel more stressed.

Well, these are the thoughts that need your utmost attention. Instead of overthinking them, write them on your journal and ponder on why they disturb you.

-Find out the Reason of Your Thoughts

It's time to find out the reasons behind your stress triggering thoughts. Take each thought that you have written on the paper and start focusing on it. Find out why you think the way you think. Investigate which experience from your past made you think this way. What part of the future (with regards to the thought) scare you most such that you have to think about it frequently?

For instance, if you are holding on to a thought that states, "I can't have an intimate relationship with someone as I don't feel comfortable sharing my thoughts with someone else" then recall the past events to find out the last time you shared something very personal with someone else and how that event affected your life.

You may find that the reason you cannot develop a close bond with someone is because the last time you did so, that person ridiculed you and made fun of your feelings. However, you aren't happy with the way you are and want to be better. The next step teaches you how to do that.

-Change Your Actions to Change the Results

Once you have figured out the reason behind your thoughts, it's time to change your actions so you don't get the same result as you did the last time. At this point, you know what actions made you overthink things and brought you stress as a result.

Now your job is to set up your routine in such a way that you don't do the same actions that made you unhappy and frustrated in the past.

Continuing with the earlier example, you slowly try to mingle with people who really understand you and first develop a bond of trust with them before sharing your personal matters with them.

Engaging in this practice on a daily basis will resolve the many troubling issues you are facing and will give you better insight into yourself. Moreover, you'll start staying at the top of your thoughts and will develop the ability to easily disengage from a stress triggering thought and focus more on the happy ones. This improves your emotional well-being and keeps you from overthinking at all times.

Next, we will discuss mindfulness based eating to increasingly make mindfulness part of your everyday practice.

Mindfulness Based Eating☐

Quite frankly, practicing breathing meditation and doing an exercise to make yourself aware of your thoughts is not enough if you want to be completely mindful all the time.

Doing the exercises discussed previously will hardly take 20 minutes of your day. Although, these 20 minutes are well spent, the effects of these exercises can be magnified throughout the day by applying other ways to practice awareness in order to stay mindful all the time.

A good strategy to cultivate mindfulness in your life is to practice mindful eating. It's a technique wherein you pay attention to your food while you're eating rather than paying attention to something else like your thoughts or watching television or talking to someone else. When you eat mindfully, you enjoy eating your food and you eat less (because you are mindful enough to detect when you have had enough), which makes you feel light and energetic all the time.

Here's how you can practice mindfulness based eating.

How to Eat Mindfully

Here is how you can eat mindfully in order to cultivate mindfulness in your routine life.

Make a habit to eat alone when you want to practice, so you don't get indulged in conversations with anybody while you are eating as doing this will only distract your mind from concentrating on the food. Also, make sure to turn off the TV and stop using the mobile while you are eating.

Take your hot plate of food and sit on the table, smell the aroma of the food and notice how its aroma is making your mouth to salivate. Notice the aroma coming from your food and try to guess the ingrecients from the smell.

Close your eyes while you take the first bite of your food; chew it slowly and try to figure out the taste of each ingredient you think it has. A good tip to eat slowly is to count until 25 while chewing before swallowing. Doing this will help you chew more, which helps you digest the food easily. This improves your digestion, which in turn improves your physical well-being.

As you swallow, try to notice the sensations you experience when the food is moving in different parts of your mouth before you swallow, just before it enters your esophagus and as it moves down until it gets to the stomach where you can no longer feel it. Taste the sensations left on your mouth just after swallowing (before taking another bite).

Now take each bite with your eyes open and chew it for at least 25 times. Feel the taste and texture of each ingredient while you chew your food and enjoy the taste of it. Complete your meal this way in silence, with no distractions around and enjoy each bite as you take it.

Keep practicing mindful eating this way until you feel that you can eat in silence even when there are people around. Eating this way will make you mindful while you are eating and at times while you are not.

Now that you have learnt how to eat mindfully to cultivate mindfulness in your life, it's time that you should learn to incorporate mindfulness in other activities that you do on daily basis in order to train yourself to stay mindful at all times.

Chapter 11: Benefits of Mindfulness

Mindful meditation has been discovered to foster the ability to inhibit those very quick emotional impulses.

-Daniel Goleman

Physical Benefits of Mindfulness

As discussed earlier Mindfulness has positive effects on reducing the stress. It is quite evident that stress leads to many physical complications along with adverse effects on mental well-being.

There are following physical benefits that one can have by practicing mindfulness.

Reducing Stress Mindfulness practice as started off from its first implementation as a stress buster therapy in MBSR program. This has shown considerable effect in reducing stress and stress induced complications. This is widely practiced by psychiatrists across the globe to treat stress. It helps in reducing stress caused by different reasons in comparatively easier way than any other therapy.

Curing Insomniac Conditions (Sleeplessness)

This concept has provided a definitive therapeutic application for those who are suffering from insomnia. It has proved to be beneficial for reducing the complications related to insomnia in different patients that have shown no improvements even by taking prolonged medications.

Reducing Hyper Tension (High blood pressure)

As it is useful in reducing the stress and relieving insomniac conditions; it helps in reducing conditions such as hypertension mainly occurring due to stress-induced causes. Practicing mindfulness brings you peace of mind and reduces the chances of hypertension.

Avoiding the Cardiac Issues Mindfulness practice is proved to be beneficial for the patients suffering from various heart ailments. It mainly works by lowering down the stress and maintaining blood pressure that accounts for increased risk of cardiac disorders. Research based studies carried out on assessing the impacts of mindfulness practice over cardiac patients indicate that those practicing these techniques have comparatively lower risk of stress induced cardiac diseases.

Relieving Chronic Pain

Practicing mindfulness helps in improving mental stamina and relieves stress. It affects the sufferer in dealing with the pains easily as compared with others. A patient with mental calm and patience can easily handle chronic pain as compared with a normal patient.

Improving Digestion (Gastrointestinal Disorders)

The chances of gastrointestinal disorders among the mindfulness practitioners are quite low as compared with others because physiological activities are at normal function and digestion and other such issues disappears easily.

Psychological Benefits of Mindfulness

Mindfulness was originally evolved for treating the psychological disorders. It is basically used as therapy in treating the different psychiatric conditions. Below are the psychological benefits of Mindfulness.

Depression

Mindfulness meditation has shown considerable effects in treating patients suffering from depression. It is an excellent way to control causes that leads to depression and helps in maintaining the mental balance of the patients with positive thought process. It reduces the stress caused by extreme and uncontrollable flow of thoughts.

Drug Addiction

Mindfulness is found to be effective in breaking the habit formation as in most of the cases for substance abuse or drug addiction occurs. It relieves the person from the different complexities caused by anxiety associated with withdrawal thereby making it easy to quite the usage of drugs.

Behavioral Issues

This is basically a therapy that is mean to treat the behavioral issues and complications. It has excellent results in treating various behavioral problems.

Anxiety Disorders

As the mindfulness practices help in controlling the though process it is one of the definitive practices to reduce the complications developing from the negative thoughts like as anxiety disorders.

Obsessive-compulsive disorder

The mindfulness meditation techniques used to stop the flow of uncontrollable flow of thoughts are quite helpful in managing compulsive conditions to a greater extent.

Mindfulness for Mental Strength

Mental Satisfaction

It helps in developing a positive attitude towards life and helps to stay calm in odds. This is quite required for a satisfactory life.

Increased Participation

Mindfulness increases your involvement in the activities at both physical and mental level that provides you the opportunities to enjoy the moments with no restrictions. This is the most critical part of being satisfied with what you have instead of getting depressed due to lack of things.

Reduced Worries

Most of the practitioners have felt that practicing the meditative techniques based on mindfulness has reduced their worries about future, career and other matters up to a larger extent.

Regarding Higher Intelligence context

Many of the practitioners engaged in mindfulness meditation have experienced something that is found to be above human considerations. The precognitions and others such abilities may also be developed in the practitioners. It is beyond the scope of this book but mindfulness has definitive effects that resembles to the ideology of Silva Mind Power and the Yoga advantages dealing in the development of the higher consciousness or higher intelligence. This is a topic that is meant for those having advanced level practice in Mindfulness.

Chapter 12: Mindfulness and Therapy

There are many different mindfulness techniques that can be utilized throughout the therapeutic process, and therapists decide on which to use based on the presenting issue (are you depressed? Anxious? Need to work through past trauma), your comfort level, and your input. Therefore, it is important to understand what is available to you and your loved ones.

The most prominent of mindfulness techniques that can also be utilized in therapy is MBSR or Mindfulness-Based Stress Reduction. This theory was pioneered by Jon Kabat-Zinn in the late 1900s in order to help others fight stress and heal their mind and body. Mindfulness-Based Stress Reduction is an intensive eight-week course that can still be taken today, in either one of the two programs that Jon Kabat-Zinn started (one at the University of Massachusetts Medical School and the other is the Center for Mindfulness in Medicine, Health Care, and Society which is also located at the University of Massachusetts Medical School). In addition to taking the eight-week course created by the founder, there are also many free online programs facilitated by fully certified MBSR instructors. The Center for Mindfulness states that it has had over 24,000 people through its program since opening in the 1970s; and Kabat-Zinn touts the following about his program: "Mindfulness-Based Stress Reduction (MBSR) is a well-defined and systematic patient-centered educational approach which uses relatively intensive training in mindfulness meditation as the core of a program to teach people how to take better care of themselves and live healthier and more adaptive lives… This model has been successfully utilized with appropriate modifications in a number of other medical centers, as well as in non-medical settings such as schools, prisons, athletic training programs, professional programs, and the workplace" (2013). These 8-week programs contain typically contain an introduction to breathing exercises, yoga, and more.

If you are looking for further ways to have a guide through mindfulness, perhaps consider finding a therapist that is able to facilitate Mindfulness-Based Cognitive Therapy or Mindfulness, Dialectal Behavior Therapy, or Acceptance and Commitment Therapy. Each of these theories contains ways to help the clients use them to become more mindful and to use that mindfulness to heal. Many therapists have mindfulness techniques in their toolbox but be careful to select one that has training in a specific theory if you are attending sessions to work on said practice. Another possibility to search for trained mindfulness coaches in your area. This can be done through a regular search, or you can navigate to the website of the

University of Massachusetts' Center for Mindfulness (https://www.umassmed.edu/cfm/) and do a search for a certified coach through their website.

How Can I Utilize Mindfulness?

We've covered how mindfulness can be utilized in therapy, but what are some ways you can work on it by yourself? There are various parts of your life that you can easily utilize mindfulness and do just about any time or anywhere, but before we get into them, there are seven things that Jon Kabat-Zinn shares that everyone who practices mindfulness should take time to note before beginning (O'Brien, 2017):

1) Don't judge. Maybe we've heard this in conjunction with others. Don't judge; be kind; give them the benefit of the doubt. Now it's time, my friend, that you start doing that with yourself. Thoughts will come up while you are practicing mindfulness. You will get distracted. That is an extremely normal happenstance within the practice of mindfulness and happens even to those who have been working on mindfulness for an extended period of time. Take a moment to notice those thoughts and where your mind goes and then gently and without judgement pull it back into the exercise.

2) Utilize the wisdom of patience. It can be easy to be pulled away and not stay in the moment and not be present. Be

patient not to rush to the next thing, but also be patient with yourself when your mind wanders. Simply pull it back gently into the exercise.

3) Trust in yourself. Building trust in yourself and a sense of trustworthiness will allow you to better engage in the process and eventually move your trust toward others and the world.

4) Be "non-doing" in your mindfulness practice. Mindfulness is not about "getting" somewhere with your practice. It is about being in awareness. Learn to be comfortable with the non-doing.

5) Let go. There is great power in letting things drift away. It can be easy to focus on a particular instance or thing that

needs to be accomplished. Take the time to let go of those things and actively engage in the mindfulness process.

6) Bring gratitude into your mindfulness. Gratitude brings joy and connectedness to others into everyday life, which will enhance your mindfulness practice.

7) Be kind to yourself. There are no "shoulds" in mindfulness. Other than you should do it. That one is a bit important.

Two additional things to keep in mind while you are starting your mindfulness practice is to:

Keep going. It takes practice to fully get into the groove. Most likely, if you are a beginner, there will be a learning curve that will take time.

Utilize mindfulness often. Once a day is a great start, but ideally, you'll get into the habit of utilizing it multiple times a day or for longer stretches.

While there are several mindfulness techniques covered here, it is strongly suggested that you utilize the additional resource section of this book for more techniques and guidance.

Mindfulness in Conversation

Do you ever have a conversation with your significant other, boss, or maybe even your child and suddenly you realize you have no idea what they are talking about because your mind wandered off? Practicing mindfulness can help you stay in the moment and to be aware of them and yourself.

Mindful Techniques for Conversation

1) Take a few deep breaths before going into a conversation, leaving your to-do list and everything else behind.

2) Note the other person's body language, this is help clue you in to how they are feeling and keep you attuned to the conversation.

3) Be present. Whenever a distracting thought comes up, push it away.

4) Tune in to the tone of their voice.

5) Try to focus only on what the other person is saying, don't formulate your next answer in your head and wait for them to finish speaking so that you can say it. Be

authentically present and allow your response to come after they have finished speaking. It's okay if your response takes a moment.

6) Give yourself grace if your mind wanders off, but pull it back in.

7) After the conversation ends, notice what went well and what did not. What can you improve on in the future? Do you feel that you gained more out of this interaction than others?

Mindful Technique for Social Media

1) Wait to engage in social media until you are in a place that you can be mindful.

2) Find somewhere comfortable to be. Think of your intentions about wanting to pull up social media.

3) Set expectations on the amount of time you will spend on social media. Set a timer if you need to do so.

4) Take a few deep breaths and notice any emotions or tightness that comes up in your body.

5) Open the social media platform of your choice and take in the first thing on your feed before you start scrolling. What do you notice? Are there any feelings attached? If there aren't, why not?

6) Continue on to the next and do the same.

7) Repeat for at least one to two more updates before continuing your regular scrolling.

8) When you are finished, take a moment to note your feelings and check-in to see how your body feels.

Chapter 13: MINDFULNESS TECHNIQUES FOR STRESS, ANXIETY AND DEPRESSION RELIEF

This chapter will show you how you can use mindfulness to deal with stress, anxiety and depression.

Mindfulness For Stress Relief

I have mentioned several times during the course of this book that mindfulness is one of the most efficient therapies for dealing with stress. Just sitting down to meditate for a few minutes can help you manage stress. Therefore, the next time you are feeling stressed, you should try mindful breathing exercises.

Find a cool and quiet place to sit or stand.

Place one hand on your chest and the other hand on your stomach.

Start breathing through your nostrils and observe the way the hand on the stomach rises and falls and how the hand on your chest moves.

Breathe out through your mouth and push out as much air as you can as you contract your abdominal muscles. When you exhale, the hand on your stomach will move a little.

Continue inhaling through your nose and exhaling through your mouth until you feel relaxed.

Get up and do some stretching after which you can go about your daily activities. You can also add some music and aromatherapy if you are in a place that allows you to do that as this would help you relax even better.

Mindfulness For Anxiety Relief

There is not one single person in the world who doesn't have things to worry about but when it overblows to a state of anxiety and panic, it becomes unhealthy for the mind and the body.

Mindfulness can help you get rid of the panic, worry and frustration by shifting your attention away from thoughts that are triggering those feelings and this will eventually alter your psychological and emotional responses and eventually help you relax.

Finger breathing is a mindful breathing technique that is very effective in helping you cope with anxiety. The next time you are feeling anxious, frustrated or worried, you should do the following:

Hold out one of your hands in front of you. This could be your right or left hand; it's up to you to choose which hand you want to use.

Now, start using the index finger of your other hand to trace the length of your thumb.

As you trace, breathe in and out.

Trace one side and breath in, trace the other side and breath out, and then count it as one breath.

Continue to do this and count each breath.

As you do this, you are able to slow down and refocus your mind from worries and troubles and this helps you become less anxious.

Mindfulness For Depression

Depression hijacks your mood and brings sad thoughts and feelings to the forefront of your mind so that your mind becomes more focused on your bad experiences while neglecting the good ones.

Mindfulness meditation can help you break this cycle so that you can overcome depression.

This simple exercise is very effective in helping you deal with depression:

Look for a straight-backed chair and sit upright with your feet flat on the floor.

Close your eyes.

In your mind's eyes, begin to imagine that you can see your breath flowing in and out of your body.

If your mind wanders, slowly bring it back to your breath.

Do the body scan meditation(Instructions are in the previous chapter}

Watch as your mind becomes calm and relaxed.

Do this meditation for 15 minutes every day to get rid of depression slowly and permanently. It would help you become a calm and happier person.

Chapter 14: How To Practice Mindfulness Meditation For Stress Relief

Mindfulness meditation is a type of meditation that calls on you to focus on your breath because the physical sensations caused by breathing are always present and thus, you can always use your breath as an anchor that helps you focus on the present moment.

The aim of all mindfulness meditation sessions, is to catch yourself drifting to the thoughts of problems in the work place, your relationship, school, health issues, academics, financial problems, and every other thing that stresses you up.

Whenever you catch yourself concentrating on things other than your breaths, simply bring your awareness back to the next breath.

Simple Mindfulness Meditation Practice For Stress Relief

Implement the following steps:

Sit comfortably: Find a sitting posture that helps you feel relaxed and comfortable for your mindful meditation. You can sit on the floor, on your bed, yoga mat, cushion, etc.

Take note of what your legs are doing: If you are sitting on a cushion, cross your legs in front of you. If you are sitting on a chair, rest the bottom of your feet on the floor.

Keep your upper body straightened: Straighten your upper body without stiffening your body. Let the natural curvature be there.

Take note of what your arms are doing: Keep your upper arms parallel to the upper part of your body. Keep the palms of your hand rested on your legs.

Soften your gaze: Let your chin drop a little and allow your gaze to fall gently downwards. You do not have to close your eyes. You can allow whatever appears before your eyes to be there without focusing on it.

Feel your breath: Bring your whole focus to the physical sensation of your breathing: the air passing through your mouth or nose, the rising and falling of your chest, or belly.

Notice when your mind wanders from your breath: Unavoidably, your attention will shift from your breaths and wander to other places. You do not need to try to eliminate or block your thoughts. If you notice your mind wandering, gently return your focus to your breath.

Practice kindness towards your wandering mind: You may have to deal with a constant wandering mind; that is normal too. Instead of trying to wrestle with your thoughts, simple observe them without having to react in any way. Simply sit and pay attention. As hard as it is to maintain such focus, come back to your breath as often as possible with neither judgment nor expectation.

When done, gently lift your gaze: If you had closed your eyes for the practice, gently open your eyes. Take some time to take note of the sounds in the environment. Take note of how calm your body feels presently. Take note of your thoughts and emotions before ending the session.

These nine steps are the most basic way to practice mindfulness meditation. If you make this practice a daily part of your life, you can derive many of the benefits of mindfulness we mentioned earlier—even if you do for as little as 5-minutes a day. Start with a 5-minutes practice and then build up from there until your sessions are as long as 30-minutes long.

Yoga And Mindfulness: Yoga Posses For Enhanced Mindfulness And Stress Relief

In this section, we will look at vital yoga poses that can help you stay more mindful and stress-free:

The Corpse Pose (Savasana)

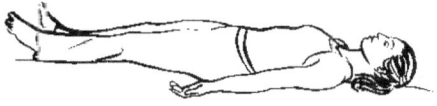

You can use this yoga pose to start and end your mindfulness yoga practices:

Steps to the Savasana:

Lie on your back and keep your feet about 12-18 inches apart and your arms at your sides a few inches away from your torso with your palms facing up.

Place your focus on your breath without attempting to manipulate your breaths whatsoever. Note an in breath for what it is and an out breath for what it is. Open up to your breath and its numerous qualities: shallow or deep, slow or fast, smooth or rough, uneven or even.

Scan your body and note if it has fully released every tension. If you feel any tension in any part of your body, visualize the tension dissipating into the air with each exhalation.

Whenever you catch your mind wandering off in thought, note the invading thought, and then bring your mind back to your breaths.

2: Eye-of-the Needle Pose (Sucirandhrasana)

This pose helps you establish mindfulness of your body, bodily sensations, and mental formations, which are all vital to stress management.

Steps to the Sucirandhrasana

From the corpse pose, bring your feet to the floor and place them near your buttocks and at hip-width apart.

Put the outer right shin on the left thigh and pull your left knee towards the direction of your chest.

Get between your legs with the right arm and around the outside of the left leg using your left arm, and keep your hands clasped.

Notice whether you restricted or held your breath as you progressed into this stretch, and continue letting the breath flow very naturally.

Depending on the openness in your body, you may feel some stretching sensations in your right hip.

You may also notice some resistance to that sensation, which will cause tensing of the surrounding muscles.

See if you can bring yourself to release this tension and observe any change in the sensation as you maintain this stretch.

3: The Cat-Cow Pose (Bitilasana and marjaryasana)

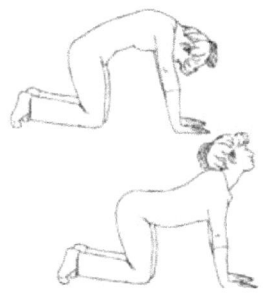

These are two yoga poses done in sequence (Bitilasana and marjaryasana)

Steps to the Cat-Cow Pose

Be on your hands and knees, have your hands directly under the shoulders and keep your knees under your hips.

As you exhale, round your back.

Let your head tilt so that you gaze back towards your thighs.

As you inhale, tilt your pelvis forward, thus opening your belly into the floor and letting your spine move into your torso thereby creating a gentle backbend.

Stretch the crown of your head and your tailbone up towards the direction of the ceiling.

Make sure you do not reach upward using your chin because doing so will compress the back of your neck.

Flow back and forth for a few breaths.

Let the timing of your breath determine your pace as you continue to coordinate your movements.

After going back and forth for a couple of times, notice your mind's ability to wander.

Come back to your breath for as many times as you catch your mind wandering to maintain the connection between your mind and body.

4: Downward-Facing Dog Pose (Adho Mukha Svanasana)

Steps to Adho Mukha Svanasana

From the Cat-Cow pose, simply tuck your toes under, lift your hips, and keep your legs straightened to get into the Down Dog.

Playfully explore this pose by bringing your heels to the floor one at a time.

Coordinate with your breath and notice if in the face of repetitions, your mind wanders off in thought.

Once you have straightened both legs, maintain that position for anywhere between 8-15 breaths.

Stay alert to body sensations, mental formations, and the way your experience continuously changes.

This posture re-creates itself moment-by-moment, breath-by-breath.

When you come out of this posture, you will notice you feel different from when you went into this posture. Some people report that after the pose, they felt like a different person altogether—no tension, no stress, and more awareness.

5: Mountain Pose (Tadasana)

The mountain pose is the foundation for all standing poses—not just something to do between other perceived more important poses.

Steps to Tadasana

Stand with your arms placed on your two sides.

Press the four corners of your feet into the ground, thus distributing your body weight evenly between your feet and centering it just in front of your heels.

Imagine your pelvis as a bowl with its rim level, both side-to-side and front to back.

Let your spine rise up, and keep your lower ribs from jutting out.

Gently lift your chest and open your heart.

Relax your shoulders.

Keep your chin parallel to the floor and your ears centered over your shoulders.

Take note of what happens as you simply stand there. Be fully awake to every sensation arising within you as you maintain this pose: the subtle swaying of your body, the sensations of your inhalations and exhalations, etc.

6: Warrior Pose 11 (Virabhadrasana)

Steps to Virabhadrasana

Reach out to your sides with your arms placed parallel to the floor and step your feet apart to keep them directly under your fingertips.

Turn in your left foot about 15 degrees and your right foot about 90 degrees.

Without leaning forward, bend your right knee toward a 90-degree angle to place the knee directly over your ankle.

Keep your arms parallel to the ground and keep gazing out over your right hand.

As you inhale, remain alert to changes in the quality of your breath, its depths, and rate.

As sensations begin to mount in your shoulders or front thigh, notice how your mind reacts.

Notice what happens to the quality of your experience if you stay with this breath while releasing every tension you feel in your body.

Notice the story lines that arise about what is happening and choose to listen without really grasping at any of them.

Rather than solidifying your sensations into the entities with which to do battle, embrace them with full awareness.

If possible, notice their habitual, non-personal nature. After doing both sides, return back to Mountain pose and scan through your entire body while staying open to whatever sensation arises.

7: Half Lord of the Fishes Pose (Ardha Matsyendrasana)

Steps to Ardha Matsyendrasana

Sit in a cross-legged position; slide the left foot under the right thigh so that your heel comes rests on the outside of the right hip.

Cross your right foot over your left thigh so that the sole of your right foot stays fully planted on the ground.

Hug the right leg using the left arm a little bit below the knees and using your right hand, press into the ground behind you.

Extend your spine upwards.

Twist to your right using your left hand to aid the left side of your body in coming around to the right.

Turn your head to your right at the end of the torso's movement and keep your neck relaxed.

Be in the present with your inhalation and exhalation, allowing it to take you through the exploration processes of release as you exhale and untwist gently. Repeat the entire process on the other side of your body.

8: Seated Forward Bend (Paschimottanasana)

Steps to Paschimottanasana

Sit with your legs straight out in front of you.

Press the back part of the thighs, calves, and the heels in the ground.

Reach through your knees and flex your toes toward your head.

Press your hands into the ground beside your hips and then lift your chest.

If your lower back rounds and your weight is on your tailbone, sit up on a blanket support.

Hold your feet or your shins, soften your groins, and turn your thighs slightly inward.

Lengthen out your torso over your legs and keep the lower back from rounding.

Let go of your grasping mind; just be where you are.

Feel your breaths move within your body.

Let yourself be in the moment of the posture, and let go of any form of clinging or aversion to the ever-changing phenomena.

When done, rest in Corpse Pose for a couple of minutes, allowing the experience of the practice to penetrate your body and mind deeply.

After the yoga exercises, all of which whose aim is to help you attain a greater level of mindfulness as a way of fighting stress, you can go straight into deep breathing meditation techniques for enhanced stress-relieving effects.

Chapter 15: Mindful exercises under 10 minutes to 30 minutes

5 Short Mindfulness Exercise You Start With

The benefits of mindfulness have made it such an important way to de-stress and maintain a good well-being in this very busy world. That is why it is a good idea to get on-board. Our minds are constantly racing, dealing with one problem then the next after it. With so much on our minds, our thoughts and feelings are left scattered. Maybe you are reading this book because it is getting too much.

The problem with mindfulness is that most of us don't have 10 minutes to sit and practice mindfulness exercise, let alone 45 minutes as recommended. If your days are as such there is no need to stress yourself over it. You can be able to squeeze in a few minutes here and there every day to practice and cultivate mindfulness. You will not be disappointed by the improvement of your mind, your emotions and your body. With just a few minutes a day you can achieve mind-body equilibrium and de-stress.

I am a busy person just like billions around the world, and so I can say I am in the majority. However, here are some simple mindfulness exercises I have learnt, mastered over the years. These have been proven to help you achieve that much required tranquility you need before, amidst and after a hectic day.

Exercise 1: Mindful Breathing

The first mindfulness exercise we will look at is called Mindful Breathing. This mindfulness technique is a very simple one and is similar of an earlier exercise (Simple Mindfulness Exercise in chapter 3: Starting on your own). This exercise can be practiced whether you are standing or breathing. This is an exercise you can do on your lunch break, before bed or anything you are alone. The fundamental of this mindfulness exercise is to stay still and remain focus on your breathing for about a minute or two.

1. Start by slowly breathing in and out. Each cycle (consisting of breathing in and out) should take about 5 seconds. Inhale through your nose and exhale out your mouth, allowing your breath to flow smoothly in and out of your body. Imagine it as a seamless cycle of flow.

2. Next empty your mind of all thoughts. Let go off your day. Let go of ongoing

projects, past projects and projects to come. Let go of wok and other things occupying your mind and just relax. Just be still for a minute.

3. Now bring your full attention to your breath and your breath along. Feel the seamless flow of air in and out of tour body. Focus on your body filling with air and life. Focus on the air moving through your nose, body and out of your mouth. Feel the energy dissipate into the world.

You can simply relax and enjoy this exercise for about 2 to 3 minutes. You should be feeling much more relaxed and in touch with the world by now. You are now a practitioner. The calm of mind gotten from meditation is a good feeling.

Exercise 2: Mindful Observation

Mindful observation is a very powerful tool you can use to relax and improve your wellbeing. It is one that has been practiced by many and have transformed their health and lives for the better. This meditation technique involves getting close to nature and appreciating it. There is so much to the world around us that we fail to see. We always have a task at hand, whether it is work, school or home. We fail to notice the world around us. Mindfully that is. Mindful observation is built on meditating on the natural world around us.

1. Pick an object in nature, it can be two ducks, a goose, a flower or even an insect. You can decide to focus on the moon or even clouds as the float by. It can be any object in your immediate surrounding. Now really notice this object.

2. You should not think about the object, just look at it closely and notice it. Relax your mind and concentrate on the object like it is your very first time of seeing this object. Notice the colors, the curves and the lines, and every detail of the object with no bias or judgement. Just visually explore this marvelous work of natural,

rediscovering every aspect of the object's formation.

3. Allow yourself to be intrigued by this object. Feel yourself connect with its essence, role and purpose in the natural universe. Take your time, if you feel yourself judging the object kindly remind yourself not to. Just enjoy the presence of the object with no judgment.

You can also examine the simple objects around you. Even a pencil can be an item of much appreciation. Just pick it up and really look at it but do not judge the object and do not wonder off.

Mindfulness is exploring, meditating and enjoying the world with no judgements what-so-ever.

Exercise 3: Mindful Awareness

This mindfulness exercise is designed to cultivate and create a heightened sense of

awareness for the simple tasks we perform around us. This similar to another describe in Chapter 3: Starting On Your Own. This exercise - Mindful Awareness is an expansion on that exercise.

Mindful awareness will allow you to have appreciation of simple daily task. You can actually get to enjoy doing every day activities and chores. Consider a daily task that you do all the time such as switching on your computer or opening a door. When you touch the door knob or the power button, stop for a second and focus on your surroundings, the emotions flowing through your mind and the sensations your body feels. Also consider the purpose of the door and where it leads to. In the same way consider the purpose of the power button and what it leads to. All of these may seem like simple things. But have you ever been mindful of these actions? Appreciate the fingers and hands that allows you to start this process, the thoughts that follows through your brain and the brain itself that allows you to think about your computer and how your brain enabled you to use it.

Mindful Awareness does not have to include only physical objects and activities. You can use them to control and relieve yourself of negative thoughts. The next time a negative thought or sensation happens, you should take a second to stop, think about it, label it as obstructive and finally let go of this negativity. Another example is when you drink a glass of water, just feel the coolness and wetness of the water flow down your throat. Appreciate the cool and quenching nature of the water. Enjoy the feeling and appreciate how privileged you are to have a cool glass of water. Also when you share a meal, take your time to smell the pleasant aroma, and appreciate the fact that you have good food and friends and family to share this experience with. You can appreciate the meal just as much alone to.

The next time you go for a walk just appreciate nature, architecture, the people, the skies, the sand, and the rocks. Just notice and embrace.

As you go through life from now on, choose touch points that resonates with you and your soul. Instead of simply rushing through life and your daily routine like a mindless zombie, take time to stop and build your purposeful awareness of the world around you, the activities you perform and the many joys these activities bring to your life.

Feel yourself de-stress.

Exercise 4: The Ten Second Count

This is a single exercise that allows you to improve upon your concentration as you become more mindful. It is a very simple exercise. Start by focusing on counting to ten. Close your eyes first, breath in through your nose and exhale through your nose, and count to 10. If you feel your mind beginning to wander, start from 1 again. Here are some thoughts that can make your thoughts wonder.

"1...2...3...4...did I remember to buy milk for tomorrow or did Mary say she would buy it? Oh, whoops, my mind wondered."

"1...2...3...4...5...this isn't so difficult in any way... Oh no....I just had another thought! Time to start again."

"1...2...3... now I've got it. I'm really concentrating on counting...That's another thought"

Keep on it until you have concentrated solely on an action simple as counting.

In the next chapter, we will look at longer mindfulness exercises.

Chapter 16: The Difference Between Meditation and Mindfulness

Oftentimes, meditation and mindfulness are discussed hand-in-hand, leading to many people not realizing that there is actually a difference between the two. This connection might arise due to the fact that there is a form of meditation known as "mindful meditation," and it is intended to bridge the two so that you can use meditation as a tool to cultivate a deeper sense of mindfulness in your life.

When it comes to awakening through mindfulness and improving your personal growth and self-esteem, understanding how each of these two tools serves you and how they can fit together to serve each other is important. Recognizing when, where, and how each one can be used is going to help you learn which tool is necessary for the job at hand, allowing you to create change effectively in your life in many different ways. Throughout this chapter, we are going to cover what each tool is, when you should use that tool, and how you can use it in such a way that it is going to give you the best results.

The Differences Between Meditation and Mindfulness

The biggest difference between meditation and mindfulness is where your awareness resideswhen you are using mindfulness or meditation as a tool and how you can use that awareness to achieve a specific result. In meditation, while you use mindfulness to help improve your practice, your primary focus is within yourself. You are focused largely on how you are feeling, what is going on inside of your body, and what thoughts you are having in your mind. Meditation is entirely focused on your experience with the world around you and how that is affecting you. Mindfulness, on the other hand, is external. With mindfulness, you are focusing on how you are experiencing the world as you perceive it, what is going on around you, and how you are being impacted by events or circumstances that are beyond your physical self.

In many cases, these two tools are interchangeable, and you can use both at the same time. In doing so, you allow yourself to turn your awareness both inward and outward, achieving a greater state of understanding of what is going on inside your head and what is going on around you and elsewhere in the world. Having both of these elements in your consciousness helps create a fuller sense of understanding of every area of your life. This way, you can create more mindful and intentional approaches to the world around you.

Everything You Need to Know About Using Meditation

Meditation itself is generally done in a seated or lying down position so that the individual can remain still and focused on their inner world. Virtually every time you engage in meditation, you are also engaging in some degree of inward mindfulness, allowing you to increase your focus on what is going on inside your head. In common meditation practices, your focus is largely on expanding your awareness, creating a state of calmness within yourself, and finding inner peace. You spend your time relaxing, breathing, and being one with yourself so that you can begin to have more integrated and peaceful experience with life itself.

There are countless types of meditation that you can engage in, each with its own set of benefits that can help you in one way or another. If you want to live a more mindful and awakened life, understanding each of these types of meditation and how they work is important. Each meditation type is going to be a tool that you can use at one point or another in your life, so it is worthwhile to understand what they are and when you can use them.

The first type of meditation that you may want to use is known as "breath-awareness meditation," and it also happens to be the most basic and common form of meditation that you can perform. Breath-awareness meditation helps you relax by allowing you to focus solely on your breath and the way your body feels each time you inhale or exhale. Many people use breath-awareness meditation on a day to day basis as a way to keep themselves relaxed and more resilient toward stressors and discomforts that life brings.

"Loving-kindness meditation" is another form of meditation that you can practice. This type of meditation allows its practitioners to send love and kindness to themselves, other people in their lives, and the world at large. It also allows you to internalize anything that you currently experience. The purpose of loving-kindness meditation is to teach yourself to have a more loving, kind, compassionate, and understanding approach to the world around you. This is a powerful form of meditation for people who find themselves frequently feeling frustrated, upset, or angry because of the different stressors that they may be experiencing in their everyday lives.

"Mantra-based meditation" is a meditation style that can help you create certain feelings within yourself and your body. Mantras are often chosen by the meditating individual based on their goal of helping themselves create a certain focus or state of awareness within. Some mantras are simple, humming sounds that have been used traditionally for generations as a way to create stillness and calmness within the body. Other mantras are affirmations that the individual chooses to repeat to themselves as a way to help them stimulate more feelings of empowerment, compassion, love, peace, calmness, affection, confidence, beauty, acceptance, or anything positivity that they desire more in their lives.

"Visualization meditations" are used for many reasons, although they are typically used to help people prepare themselves for new or significant life experiences. For example, if you are preparing for an important career meeting that you have been waiting for, visualization can help you prepare yourself for the meeting by giving yourself a clear focus of what you want to accomplish and how you are going to accomplish it. You can also use visualization to improve your skills, socialization abilities, confidence or self-esteem, your happiness, and many other things. You can also use it to attain and maintain overall peace in your life.

"Guided meditations" are used for many different experiences. Its benefits overlap with that of visualization meditations. You can use guided meditation to improve your inner peace, help you sleep, prepare you for something important, or even to visualize what you want more in your life using a tool called "manifesting." Guided meditations can be used by following a guided YouTube meditation or audio meditation or by visiting a meditation specialist who can guide you through a live in-person session as you meditate.

When it comes to meditation, you need to be prepared to set aside some time for your meditative experience. This way, you have enough time, energy, and attention to engage in your meditation and gain your desired benefits from it. You should always have an intention or goal when going through your meditation experience, as this will help keep you focused and give you a reason for showing up in your meditation sessions. The reason for meditating for many is as simple as "I want to feel more relaxed right now." Having a reason for engaging in your meditation helps you create a purpose that you can be mindful of, allowing you to integrate mindfulness into your meditation experience. As a result, no matter what form of meditation you engage in, you will also be actively exercising and strengthening your mindfulness abilities.

Everything You Need to Know About Using Mindfulness

Mindfulness is entirely focused on your state of awareness and where you place your focus. This includes the practice of meditation itself, but it also includes your everyday life and the experiences that you have about the world. Being in an active state of mindfulness ultimately means that you are focusing on your thoughts, feelings, behaviors, and movements. You are also focusing on how you are affecting the world around you and how the world around you is affecting you.

You can engage in a mindfulness practice anytime, regardless of where you are, who you are surrounded by, and what is going on around you. When you are being mindful, you are paying attention and noticing everything about the present moment, regardless of whether or not you perceive it to be good or bad. This is a powerful state to be in, as it differs from how the average person lives their day to day lives. Most people go through their lives mechanically and doing everything because they have to and because it is what they have always done. They succumb to their efficient brains and habits, and then they simply engage in these habits over and over again. This way, rather than having to put the energy and effort into actively thinking about what they are doing, they can just do it on autopilot and let their minds be at rest as they go about their day. For a person who is being mindful, this looks entirely different.

Conclusion

Mindfulness is more than just meditating to improve your concentration and clarity – it is a practice through which thousands of people have taken back control of their minds and bodies. By practicing mindfulness meditation you can increase your awareness of your thoughts and emotions, working through the negative ones and letting them go to make room for the positive. The more you practice mindfulness meditation, the more you will experience its benefits. If you suffer from chronic stress, anxiety, depression, or pain, spending just a few minutes a day in mindful meditation can make a world of difference.

In reading this book you have received a wealth of information about what mindfulness is, how it can benefit you, and how to go about practicing it. Hopefully by the time you finish this book you have cultivated a deep understanding of mindfulness meditation and you see its potential to benefit you and those around you. If you are ready to take control of your thoughts and emotions, choose one of the mindfulness exercises in this book and try it for yourself. You will not be disappointed!

www.ingramcontent.com/pod-product-compliance
Lightning Source LLC
Chambersburg PA
CBHW072003070526
44583CB00015B/1319